Encouraging Words

by G Helen Bolton

Illustrations by G. Helen Bolton.

Published by
Bolton Publishing LLC

Foreword

I believe that God blesses us so that we may be a blessing to others. He also comforts us so that we may comfort those who are in trouble. I wrote these poems when I was under extreme duress. I revisit them often to remind me: "Do not focus on problems, but on the Lord, who can solve them."

Every day we are faced with the choice: to speak in faith or in fear. A *fearful* man says, "God, look how big this mountain is that is blocking my path." A *faithful* man says, "Mountain, do you realize how *big* my God is? You better get out of the way if you want to live to see another day."

I hope that as you read these meditations, you will be encouraged to see your way through the obstacles in your path.

References: II Corinthians 1:3-4, Mark 11:22-23.

Table of Contents

Encouraging Words

When I dropped by to visit a friend, I shared with her what I had just written. She said, "You wrote that for me. You just do not know how much I needed that today." I smiled because I had desperately needed it the day before.

I am so glad that we spent time together giving our problems to God and encouraging one another. It amazes me how You can use me to write words that inspire, yet still express my heart's desires. It is a blessing to be so blest, to be able to write down what you hold dear, so when others hear, they have no fear.

Reassured that You are in command and have the victory close at hand, we survey the land. With You by our side, we take our stand. Words really do have the power to build us up or wear us down.

Sometimes it is more important to be silent than to speak. While at other times, we must press on rather than retreat. But it is never best to sow seeds of agitation, fueled by anger and frustration.

I want the words that I have said, that will live on after I am dead, to be words of inspiration and meditation, words of hope and reconciliation. Words that let others know: "You love them so."

References: Proverbs 15:23; Psalm 19:14; 2 Corinthians 1:3, 4; Isaiah 30:8; Habakkuk 2:2; Matthew 12:33-37; John 3:16; Romans 5:8

A Frown or a Crown?

What are you going to wear today? Do not be dismayed and wear a frown when you can reign with Jesus and wear a crown. The spirit of offense is like meat in a trap that lures you closer before the attack.

Negative words are seeds that develop roots of bitterness that zap us of our strength and cheerfulness. The weeds that they sprout have bitter roots whose purpose is to distract and pollute. Their seeds bear fruit after their own kind, trying to enslave all of mankind. Be sure those seeds fall on rocky ground. Cast them down. Do not be discouraged and wear a frown. You were meant to wear a crown. Go to where the Rock of your Salvation is found. Walk with Him on holy ground, where His mercies abound all year 'round.

You are a child of the King. You should joyfully sing, 'Through Christ I can do all things! Hosanna to the King of kings!' Let us sing it again and again. Let us say, "Amen" and "Amen."

References: Philippians 4:13; Psalm 95:1; Matthew 21:9, 16; Genesis 8:22; Revelation 17:14; Mark 4:24; Hebrews 12:15; 13:20-21

No Wonder

Father,
You have begun a good work in my heart.
Right from the start, You cleansed every part.
But You won't stop until You make me perfect,
    complete, lacking no good thing.
No wonder men and angels sing,
  "Hosanna to the King of kings!"

    References: Philippians 1:6; John 12:13;
Revelation 17:14

For the Master

Father, thank you for Your loving kindness.
You helped me overcome my blindness.
You opened my eyes, so I could see what really
    matters to me.
You help me each step of the way, waiting patiently
    for me to stop and pray.
You even help me know what to say!

    Be honest, but stick to the facts.
    Do not lose your temper.
    Hold your tongue, and keep your peace.
    Come to Me to seek relief.
    Some things are better left unsaid;
    Choose good seeds to plant instead.

Dear Child,
Remember to give your best to the Master.
Isn't pleasing Me what you're really after?
Who are you serving, God or man?
Remember all is under My command,
and the victory will be close at hand.

References: Matthew 13:15-17; Luke 16:13; Genesis 8:22; Romans 8:31-35, 37-39

Heart and Soul

Father, I am keeping my mind on the truth that will set me free. I refuse to pay attention to the evil done to me. I will not nurture the seeds of discontentment. For I have learned the secret to contentment is to stay by Your side. With You, I can take everything in stride.

I choose to focus on the Light that brings to fruition the good seed sown into my heart and soul. As You prune away any branches that are fruitless, engraft Your Word here in my heart. Write it on my mind, and work it into my will. Let it bear fruit according to Thy will. I gladly give You my emotions and all my devotion.

You keep me in Your perfect peace because we often meet at Your Retreat. Where the heat cannot touch us, the fire cannot scorch us, the rain cannot soak us, and the ice cannot freeze us. Nothing can beat us. Right here at Jesus's feet. Consumed by the power of Your love, You joined our hearts and souls, redeemed me and made me whole. You blessed me with more love than my heart could contain. You have fulfilled more promises to me than my mind can explain. I gladly acclaim, "The Lord Reigns! Blessed be His name."

Reference: John 3:32, 8:12, 15: 2, 5, 16, 24; 1 Corinthians 13:5; Philippians 4:11; Isaiah 26:3, 43:2; Romans 5:5, 8:31, 38, 39; Psalm 113:2; Luke 19:38

'A Word in Due Season'

Father, I come to lay my burdens down and pick up my crown. I fear I have fallen to the ground with no one else around to help me up. I am drowning in a sea of despair, and I feel the need to spend this hour in prayer. I know better than to sow seeds of fear and doubt, but I am so angry I want to shout:

Satan, clear out! Praising God is what this is all about. I refuse to listen to your lies. All you ever do is criticize, and you never ever apologize! God is my Strength and my High Tower. His Word is my Sword. His faithfulness is my Shield. He is the One to whom I yield. Nothing you have said is worth repeating.

It is time to regroup and stop retreating. I put on God's armor, and take a stand, because my life is under God's Command. Father, help me sow good seed today. Help me remember to pause and pray:

Lord, please show me the Way! Forgive me for my unbelief. I have come to You to seek relief. Forgive me for being overcome with grief and for speaking in disbelief. I cannot believe this is happening to me, but I know You shape my reality. I trust Your Truth to set me free and to control my destiny.

Reference: Proverbs 15:23; Psalm 91:4

'How Sweet It Is!'

Father, I know Your Word is incorruptible and that You are certainly capable of working this out to bring me good. Even though it does not seem like I should, I will persevere, because I know it was good seed that You sowed. Even though Satan tossed in some weeds, Your words will prevail in truth and deed. They will cause Your plans to succeed. This I know, because You told me so, through Your Word written long ago. It was already established when it was written. It only needs time to come to fruition.

What I failed to realize is that time is on our side, because in You I abide. It does not matter who is against me, because You are for me. You love and adore me. I am the apple of Your eye. I will remember the battle is not from You, but the victory certainly is. I surrender my will to You, the Lord of all. With Your help, I'll recover from this painful fall. Thank you, Father, for comforting me, and assuring me, 'You know the plans You have for me, plans to prosper me and not to harm me, plans to give me a hope and a future.' I keep on asking, seeking, and knocking. You keep on giving, revealing, and opening doors. It is no wonder that You are the One I love and adore! I want to know You more and more.

References: 1 Peter 1:23; Romans 8:28; Luke 7:9; Psalms 27:8, 105:4; Matthew 7:7, 13:1-23, 24-30, 36-43; Isaiah 55:11, 54:15; Deuteronomy 32:10-11; Jeremiah 29:11 NIV; 2 Chronicles 20:15; Proverbs 15:23

During the Silence

Father, I realize there are times when I am impatient and want an answer right now. But I know some things just cannot be rushed, like baking bread or ripening fruit. There is just no substitute, for taking the time to let bread rise twice, or for leaving tomatoes on the vines until they are plump, juicy, and ripe. Hurry the process, and neither tastes right. Help me enjoy those periods of time that stretch my faith and test my determination. Waiting is not only a time of rest, but also a time of contemplation. A time to test my motives and search my heart, to be sure I have given You every part.

I need those quiet times even though, at times, I get discouraged when the answer is delayed or the price seems too high to pay. Your Spirit brings Your Word to mind, and rekindles the hope that I forgot was mine.

Your Word has never failed me, and it will not fail me now. It will prevail and reach me somehow.

You already press it down and shake it up, so You cannot pour any more into my measuring cup. So I will wait quietly, patiently, simply enjoying the pleasure of Your company.

References: Psalms 27:13-14; 40:1-3

All Day

I cherish those times when an hour of prayer is just not enough, when it takes all day just to find the right words to say, the right words to pray.

Thank you for being patient as You watch me grow, and lovingly showing me the way to go; for taking the time to stretch my faith, and for adjusting Your pace to match my small gait.

Thank you for giving me wisdom beyond my years and helping me stand and face my fears. Thank you for giving me the measure of faith every day and the intense desire to pray.

I keep on asking, seeking, and knocking. You keep on giving, revealing, and welcoming. I keep on receiving, finding, and running through the door. You greet me with open arms and sweep me off the floor. You shower me with blessings and rainbows galore. No wonder, You are the One that I love and adore. Lord, how I want to know You more and more.

Reference: Matthew 7:7-11

8

Gratitude

Father, thank you for sending Your Son to redeem my soul and make us one. Thank you for teaching me how to pray and showing me the Way to live the abundant life every day. Thank you for the lessons that I have learned; though often difficult for my finite mind to grasp, because You care, they are mine at last.

I understand Your Word and hold it dear because Your Spirit has opened my eyes so I can see and my ears so I can hear. I consider Your Word an awesome treasure whose value is beyond all measure. I believe that You hear every word I say, so I guard my tongue night and day. I love You and my neighbor because You loved me first. I long for the day when You will quench my thirst. I forgive because I have been forgiven, and I give thanks for this abundant life that I'm living. I must remember to be humble, or I will surely stumble.

On negative thoughts I choose not to dwell because You have taught me well. From the beginning, You created seeds that bear fruit after their own kind, so it is best to keep Your Word in mind all the time. I owe You my gratitude for shaping my attitude.

References: Mark 4:23, 24; Matthew 5:6, 12:37; 1 John 4:19; Philippians 4:4-8; Ecclesiastes 3:11; Genesis 8:22

In Your Remembrance

Keep Me in your remembrance.
State your case before Me.
Trust Me to remove any hindrance that blocks your
    path, and you will know a peace that will last.
Put it on the back burner away from the flame.
You've done nothing to bring yourself shame.

Walk forward with your head up tall.
Remember Jericho's walls?
They came tumbling down when the people praised
    God as they walked around.
Gideon's army defeated Midian when his men
    praised God with their arms upraised and their
    lamps ablaze.

What can we learn from the battles they have won?
Every time we kneel in prayer,
    we acknowledge God is everywhere.
Spend time with God.
Listen to His commands,
    and the victory will be close at hand.

References: Isaiah 43:26; Philippians 4:4-8;
Isaiah 54: 16-17; Judges 7: 15-21; Joshua 6:12-16;
II Chronicles 20:15; 2 Corinthians 4:8-9, 17-19

Adonai, My LORD, I often go to our secret place, far away from life's hectic pace where I can rest from the race and talk with You face to face. I bow down in awe of Your redeeming grace. Though it cannot be proven, to me it's a fact. When I walk with You, I am on the right track and safe from any attack. I will not grow weary of doing good, nor faint in believing as I should. You started me going in the right direction and placed over me divine protection.

I had read that verse at least a hundred times, but when I read it today, it suddenly rhymed, and its rhythm even matched mine. I knew what it meant, as sure as I knew it was heaven-sent. I do not know why it did not speak to me until now, but I know it touched me and how.

It gave me the courage to persevere without fear because I knew that You were near. To send such love into the heart of man is more than I can comprehend. But this one thing I do understand, "Because You love me, my life is grand."

References: Psalm 91; 2 Timothy 3:16; Isaiah 54:15-17; Galatians 6:9

Twice Blessed

I think, "It is more blessed to give than to receive,"
because "It is a blessing to be a blessing."

Reference: Acts 20:35b KJV

Confirmation

Father,

Right after I asked You for confirmation concerning my perception of a certain situation, You placed two people in my path: one a dear friend who said, "Yes" to my request. The other a new friend who needed to hear, "You are her helpmeet, and You love her dearly."

I gave her a prescription to help her heart heal, "Read these words daily especially when You pause to pray. You need to hear them every day. When they become part of your heart, you will know His peace and find relief."

I had my confirmation by two witnesses; I was where You wanted me to be. I placed my trust in Your Master Plan, and once again, placed my life in Your nail-scarred hands.

I don't know if they realized, they helped me as much as I helped them, but they did. Because of them, my burden was lighter, and my day was brighter.

Don't you agree that is the way it's supposed to be?

References: Proverbs 3:5, 6; Jeremiah 29:11-13; Deuteronomy 19:15; John 10: 27-29; Ecclesiastes 4:9-12

Be Good!

Do not grow weary of doing good,
    of loving your brothers and sisters as you should,
    of bearing one another's burdens,
        sharing the weight of the load,
    of loving God,
        and doing what you are told.

Do not become weary of doing as you should,
    but overcome evil with good.
Don't let the spirit of offense invade your heart.
Give your troubles to God right from the start.
Remember His Word,
    not the lies you have heard.

As you walk this sod,
    recount the promises of God.
Love God's law,
    cherish His Word,
    and you will know Peace.

As you kneel before God,
    if you are humble,
Nothing shall offend you
    or cause you to stumble.

References: Galatians 6:9; James 4:10

Glorious

Isn't it glorious? Our God is victorious!
We can sleep because He watches over us.

References: 2 Corinthians 2:14; Psalm 4:8;
Proverbs 3:24

Weighed Down?

Don't take things so personally! Weigh events in the light of eternity. Ask yourself:
"How much will it matter then?"
"Does it really make a difference?"
"What can I learn from this experience?"
When you put things in the proper perspective, you will find yourself calm, cool, collected, and objective.
Don't be carried away by your emotions, and always make time for your daily devotions.

Reference: Philippians 4:11

A True Ring

You are the Potter who shaped me into a living vessel. The fire of Your Spirit has tempered me. When You thumped me the other day, You could tell I had not taken the time to pray. So You put me back in the oven until I was strong, and ready to sing a new song. You replaced the thud with a holy ring and filled me with Your love and this new song that I sing. You made me a true work of Your hands. It's no wonder why I love You and my fellowman. You live in my heart and make me strong. You gave me hope and the words of this song. I want to thank You all the daylong. Amen.

Reference: Isaiah 64:8

Perfect Peace

Dear Father,
When my burden is more than I can bear,
I give them to You on the wings of my prayers.
Songs of praise fill the air displacing my despair
    with the love we both share.
I think about the words of the songs and soar on the
    melodies to where I belong with my heavenly
    Father who makes me strong.
Just being in Your presence fills my heart with joy,
    displacing my fears with sweet communion so
    dear.
I enter Your rest knowing I am blest.
For these special times, I thank you.

Reference: Psalm 32:7

The Secret Place

Good morning, LORD. The Sun of Righteousness rose to greet me this morning. His wings brushed away the sleep from my eyes as His Light ushered in the dawn of a wonderful new day. I bask in the Light of Your presence in complete joy, secure in the Secret Place of the Most High. I cast off the worries of yesterday, today, and tomorrow. I put on Your Armor of Light: Your truth, peace, righteousness, faith, salvation, and Your Living Word. Because I am Your child, You sent the Holy Spirit into my heart filling me with Your Love, Peace, and Joy.

I had known since I was a small child that You lived in my heart, but I had never even dreamed that You would want me to live in Yours. When You invited me into Your Secret Place, into Your Heart, my joy overflowed in tears. I felt so loved, so close, and so special. I came home to dwell in You, where nothing could ever separate me from Your Love. Thank You for knowing me so well, and loving me so much that You sent Your Word just so we could keep in touch.

References: Psalms 91:1 KJV; Isaiah 26:3; Romans 8:38-39; Matthew 6:33-34; John 1:1, 14, 17; 20-21, 26; Malachi 4:2; Ephesians 3:17, 6:10-18

An All-Time Low

If you take the 'Word' out of the 'World,'
    all that remains is *l*.
If you take 'God' out of 'Good,'
    all that remains is *o*.
If you take the 'Lord' out of the 'World,'
    all that remains is *w*
Put the three together, and it spells *low*,
But with *God* by our side and His *Word* in our hearts,
    life in this '*world*' is '*good*.'

View from the Mountain Top

Father God, I am standing at the base of this mountain. I cannot find the path carved in the rock by Your Word so long ago. I know I am too weak to climb this mountain alone, but I know Your strength is made perfect in weakness. I know I can reach the mountain summit with You as my guide.

When the path is dark, Your Word lights the way. When the night is cold, the Fire of Your Spirit warms me and draws me closer to Your side. When I am tired and weary, I rest my head on Your shoulder. You soothe my brow as You give me Your sweet sleep.

Climbing this mountain with You by my side shouldering the weight of my load, I know that we are more than able to scale these lofty heights. You guide me each step of the way. When the slope is too steep for me, I see Your hand reaching down to me. I lift my hand to You, and You firmly grasp it lifting me higher from glory to glory. You make my feet surefooted as the mountain deer as together we climb the high places.

The mountain summit is mine for You have given me the victory. I say to this mountain, "By the Grace of God your heights no longer loom over me. You have lost your power over me, and my ears are deaf to your taunts and cries. I hear only the voice of my Savior saying 'Isn't the view from the mountain top glorious? I knew you would make it to the top because you are now and ever more shall be one with the Father, Spirit and Me!' "

References: Mark 11:25-31; 2 Corinthians 12:9; Psalm 119:105; Matthew 26:41-42; Romans 8:3; Matthew 11:28-30; John 1:12-14; Romans 8:9, 26, 8:28; Habakkuh 3:19-20; Joshua 1:3; Romans 8:32; Luke 10:19; Galatians 5:22-25; I John 4:18; Philippians 1:6; 2 Timothy 1:12; I Corinthians 13; Colossians 6:4; Hebrews 13:15; Psalm 100; I John 4:19; Acts 17:25; Ephesians 3:17; John 10:14; John 17:21-21; 2 Corinthians 3:18; Galatians 3:3

www.ingramcontent.com/pod-product-compliance
Lightning Source LLC
Chambersburg PA
CBHW062115040426
42337CB00042B/3675